REFLECTIONS OF A FERAL MOTHER

REFLECTIONS OF A FERAL MOTHER

Cynthia Robinson Young

WALNUT STREET
—PUBLISHING—

REFLECTIONS

OF A FERAL

MOTHER

Cynthia Robinson Young

ISBN: 978-1-967230-01-3

*The cover art is a photo of a mural created by local artist Shaun Larose.
"The Glass Street Mural: From One Generation to Another" is located
on Glass Street and Chamberlain Avenue in Chattanooga, Tennessee.
The poet was honored to sit in as the model for this monument to the
community. You can find the artist at www.shaunlarose.com.

Walnut Street Publishing
1673 S Holtzclaw Ave
Chattanooga, TN 37404

*For my sons, Benjamin, Daniel, Wesley, Isaiah, and Seth—
and my grandsons, Jaiden, Jaron, Kamran, Elias, Jonah, Davin,
Jonathan, Judah, Kyngston, and Chance*

Feral: Fierce. Tigerish. Unbroken.

When my African professor,
while reading her hometown newspaper, muttered,
    "We must do something about Feral Women,"
It was not a term I'd heard before.
Did she mean me?
Because, I am just
a woman who made
a fierce promise
on the birthing bed, passed down in the DNA
of a Mother.

TABLE OF CONTENTS

CAUL BABY

He was born in warm trust of thigh,
    sliding out
from oceans
of emerald water, feral
    and untethered,
my sac, an amniotic boat
    sailing
on a tidal wave, a quest to find his mother,
taking the same path, I took,
    traveling
from my mother's womb,
    landing on
this side of this world.

THE FIRST TIME

Two events I always confuse,
as if they happened
on the same day
when I was five years old, living
in a house we had moved away from
when I was four.

A little white girl I called
my friend;
a playground swing set
in her backyard:

My little playmate, come out and play with me
And bring your dollies, three
Climb up my apple tree... *

I played
whatever she wanted, but the one time
I didn't, she called me
the *N-Word*
and dismissed me,
pointed me back
to my house next door.

I remember sadness
sitting in my mother's kitchen
covering the sun with troubled clouds
when I asked her
what that word meant.

Then there's the second event:
Me, on the same afternoon, back
on the neighbor's swing, flying
        high
as if no mean words
were ever said—

My dress is white like the clouds,
the clouds like cotton candy,

the sky a blues baby in which
             I soar,
my brown legs pumping
high in the air, but
my dress

is now stained red,
bleeding from a word
made into a weapon
to pierce my spirit,

a violent slaughter,
a premonition
of all the future
times I will forget
to remember
to guard my
heart.

*Children's handclapping song

NOT JUST TO HAVE THE BLUEST EYE

-From Toni Morrison

In the way that it seems only females are judged,
how they descend on a scale, rated at birth,
and evaluated as the months and years go by,
how we let males judge us, how we then judge each other,
how we judge our own selves
from pretty to ugly, at twelve years old,
she had done the opposite,
beginning as Pecola Breedlove, believing herself the worst.
If someone had actually told her she was ugly then,
she couldn't remember now.
But on those late August summer days
when even the minutes on the clock
ticked time away slowly, as if too hot to move,
when the sun just sat fanning itself in the sky,
and the neighbor girls didn't have the energy to do anything else
but sit on the porch and stick out their arms, line them together,
and compare the hues of color, a contest with winners
a competition to be the lighter than a brown paper bag,
she knew whose skin was the darkest
before the others began bickering over who was the lightest,
the Winner.
She didn't even have to look--
She already knew.

And fifty years later, when her hue was finally celebrated,
when she could feel free to wear color unashamed
of what it might magnify, when she could
feel fine being the color
of dark roast coffee, no cream,
she now saw herself too old to be seen, rated,
evaluated and treasured. She saw only one color now;
the color of an old woman—
grey, white-haired, glass eyed, a ghost.

I WAS RAISED TO BE INVISIBLE

...to be seen but not heard,
to try to hide under the covers from
The Boogeyman
waiting in my closet, or under my bed--

I was raised to not go with strange men
even if I called them, "Uncle";
to walk away from love after the first slap,
the first "Baby I didn't mean it, but
it *was* your fault."

I was raised to be a good daughter,
to not take up too much air,
to do what I was told without talking back;
and so I sat in that barber's chair
for "a facial", and I, hungry for perfection,
let him put his hands on my teenage face
covered with perceived imperfections,
all distorted in the bathroom mirror.
Yet, I didn't imagine this, didn't want
his hands to roam down
to my breasts, barely budding.

But I was born with Black girl magic,
with the power to leave
that room,
that relationship,
that chair,
To run from those boogeymen,
To be strong enough to tell,
To use my voice...

To scream.

FOR DEAD MOLESTERS, WHOSE SECRETS WE KEPT

-after William Evans

Pray for those who art not in heaven
though the preacher promised them they would be
as they lay in front of the church,
rigor mortis, stone cold dead, but made up
to look like the mug shot we gave
the Undertaker.

Question if our forgiveness for their sins
against us, against our bodies, against our childhood
will actually free them of the atrocities
we can recant if we try
not to suppress them.

Who will deliver us from their evil
If they took the evil with them,
and didn't' admit and release it, like the thief
on the wrong side of the crucified Jesus,
still hanging onto his cross of unbelief?

The power was never something we possessed,
Though we yearned for its voice.

May we rest in peace.

THE RAINBOW CHILD

-for Ben

He wants God to unravel
that brown mass of curls
blanketing his small scalp.
He wants them to lie flat like
    limp spaghetti.

He wants his skin to lighten
in the sun,
to peel away the golden skin and find
    pinkness underneath.

He wants his eyes like jewels--
not coffee beans warming in the sun,
but radiant stones of aquamarine
    light and translucent.

Yet,
when the fabric of life is harsh and wrinkled,
he leans upon the bosom that suckled him,
pressing against his mother,
trying to lose himself in her black flesh.

But,
when life is ironed and folded back neatly into its familiar creases,

He rises—
stretching tall his short brown limbs
trying to reach the
        aquamarine stones,
        the strawberry spaghetti,
        the fire-red beard,
        the long pink flanks of arms and legs
as they stride a bit ahead of him.

He only wants what most little boys want.

He wants to be like his father.

MOBOLAJI

They say mothers can leave an imprint on their children
even before they are born. My son was imprinted with my trauma
of his grandmother's death, with "Botox" lines between his infant
eyes,
as if he spent most of his months in utero swimming in worry,
wondering how we would know how to be
without my mother, who had already made plans
to come to California to care for him, even while
she was being haunted by voices warning her
to put her house in order at the same time.

I was carrying him in my womb when I viewed my mother in her
casket,
her body, her face at rest, all of her worries transferred,
inherited by me, passed on to my son. So even in play,
the darkness of his depression lurks like a security blanket,
and the Nigerian name that was supposed to be a blessing
to remember he was born into riches, mocks his poverty
of joy.

MANCHILD

A boy told me/ if he roller-skated fast enough/ his loneliness couldn't catch up to him.

From "The Rider" by Naomi Shihab Nye

I wonder if that's what my son thinks,
why he walks so fast through
through the neighborhood streets
and alleys of St. Elmo,

almost like The Flash-but my son
is not a superhero.
Does he think he can beat the dark shadows
chasing, nipping at his heels, like

a Chihuahua, all bark, little bite?
If he'd only
Turn around.
Stop.
Catch
his breath, cold vapors forming

Words into an SOS, he'd see
I'm trying to catch
up to him

to read his message.

INHERITANCE

The first time he tasted condensed milk
he tasted his addiction.
He thought he tasted his mother,
but she fed him from a bottle,
and kept her pert, young breasts to herself.

She kept his addiction going,
recreated the "high" with the sugar-
sweet white crystals
that transformed into Pralines, into
sugar cookies stored
in a pink ceramic pig, a gift
she'd been given by a neighbor
for surviving at 14,
her family shame at his conception,
and his high-risk birth.

But neither survived his addiction
to the sweetness of the Crack infested streets,
offered, on corners and back alleys,
a thumping through his veins. He chose
the freedom of the immediate rush, the shock
of instant euphoria.

she forever assumed
he'd staggered into danger,
and fell in, dying somewhere
 at the feet of his addiction,
disappearing
like his great uncle
in a chain gang,
or like his great-grandfather,
dangling from a tree in Georgia-
no witnesses except the trees
 to testify.

His mother kept the pig jar for 60 years,
toting it from her cold-water flat

to the kitchen in a housing project,
guarding the pink ceramic
as if she were keeping safe a living thing,
a shrine she would leave for someone else to fill,
a juxtaposition
of freedom, strongholds
and addictions-
All roads leading

to some sort of death.

HE HAD A DREAM, Part I

-for my cousin

1.
He was supposed to be bound for glory. He had "mad skills".
He paid his dues on the football field. With spatial awareness he ran through
And past the dealers, past the drugs when he saw his sisters didn't.
Rising up on both sides, like dirty city snow,
sidestepping the Boone's Farm, the Budweiser, the Johnny Walker Red,
he was running toward the goal line. The scouts saw his future,
the coach promised his success. Fifth in the city, he was more than ready to save
his family.

2.
His mama was so sweet, there was no way he would fumble this.
He couldn't—a favorite because he was a boy among sisters,
he took his place, using his swiftness to run into danger
to get them out of it, muscled up to fight and protect this house
always gravitating
toward the darkness of the streets, toward the sirens racing toward shootings, shooting ups,
until they sang the song of the streets.

3.
It was the 1970's.
He was not supposed to get locked up.
Slavery was over. Chain gangs were over. Crack was not on the streets.
He never sold one drug.
And he even had a ticket to ride out of Newark, out of South Orange Avenue, out and away
from the sirens that wouldn't let him do his math, write his papers, wouldn't let him sleep,
and eventually

wouldn't let him live.

JUST ANOTHER WAY

"Convict Leasing-a horrific system in which Black people convicted of largely social crimes that applied only to them, were leased to private businesses who forced them to labor."-The EJI Legacy Museum

It is not appropriate that
my family was so ashamed
we had a great uncle
in a Chain Gang--
that we should try to bury it,
as if it was his fault
that in 1898, state revenue came
from convict leasing,
that it was just another way
to hold on to Black men
after slavery was abolished
but their services
were
still
needed.

GOTTA BE GRATEFUL

-for Ben

"You make sure you get back home alive."

It is a command,
an instruction,
a prayer
a part of Home Training--
those words taught, even if not habitually spoken
from every feral mother's heart.

I gotta be grateful that my son was in California
In 1992
when the police looked down at him sitting
on the ground and said to the suburban shopper,
who called security and reported him.
"Is he the one?"

I gotta be grateful that my son has white friends.
The fact that his friends were all doing the same thing—
making an action-packed testosterone video for school,
might have helped him some.
They had his friends do the explaining,
showed the po-lice
their guns weren't real,
while my son held his head down,
his wrists handcuffed together
like the shackles of his ancestors.

They let him go with
a restraining order.

So, I gotta be grateful it wasn't
a restraining rope
in a community square
in Alabama
in 1892

THE WALNUT STREET WALKING BRIDGE-Chattanooga, Tennessee

They thought.

They thought, in the year of 2010 they could
close the bridge and recreate it,
paint it Haint blue to keep its evil past away,
dedicate it to wash away its sins.

But the generations of Black Chattanoogans will not
forget what happened on the night of March 19th in 1906.
And the Elders still say it is haunted, still say
that on foggy nights, they can see Ed Johnson hanging
from the noose he wore for the crime he bore:
the violation of a white woman. the payment:
a convenient Black man.
A prisoner of mob law, he was noosed at the jail,
and dragged to the bridge.

Now, on stormy nights when the river is restless,
the Elders say they can hear the splash of his blood cutting water,
and on the fourth of July,
amid the fireworks celebrating freedom,
they hear the fifty-five gunshots
forgiving the murderous mob,
last words choked out,
a benediction echoing across all these years

"God bless you all.
I AM an innocent man."

If all that is needed to be my Judge,
Jury, and Executioner is to be a different color,
to speak a different language,
to have different ideas,
to believe in a God *you* cannot see,
then
I could be a gory decoration a mob left abased
and hanging from a Poplar tree hidden

in a forest, or dangling from
a cursed bridge in the middle of a city
for even children to see.

I could be
Ed Johnson.

TO BE A DISTANT SON

*-for Tyre Nichols, Ahmaud Arbery, and all the Black sons from
the past and the future*

1.
You can still see slavery when you shield your eyes
and look back at the not-so-distant past.
People who knew your people

have not been dead that long. You can still go back
and walk where your grandmother's grandmother walked.
There are plantations with slave shacks

standing as a reminder. Grandma Theosa talked about
the place where she lived as a child,
as if she made up Damascus, but it still exists,

where very horrific tale she told you is whispered
there among the trees that are still standing,
living witnesses of her truth.

And if she could return, her stories
could resurrect themselves, ghostly tales
lying in wait for her return, reenactments

that would chase her away from Georgia again
before they reclaimed her life
and buried her.

It doesn't matter what Damascus has become.
In Theosa's memory, the old town
she lived in, the way it was in 1918, is still there,

a community of Black folk struggling just like her,
and the white folks they tried, for safety's sake,
to stay invisible.

2.
That Theosa's grandsons, so many times removed,

would possess the same fear, would be obsessed
with the same mission—to stay safe,

might have discouraged her from even migrating.
Would this knowledge have alerted her to
the lie that we could escape this darkness?

That the evil of the human heart
would also follow the North Star,
would listen to the sound of the river?

3.
It is not a good thing to realize
you have no super power.
You are not invisible.

You are just biding time, like riding
on a Lionel train, looping
around southern towns and northern cities,

cotton plantations and high-rise Projects,
still migrating, still
searching for
that elusive
safe space.

"LET HIM GO! THAT'S MY SON!"

April 19, 2020, Harlem, N.Y.— "cell phone video shot yesterday at the 145-street subway platform in Harlem shows a group of NYPD police officers terrorizing a little boy for allegedly selling candy."

Tweeted @DrRJKavanagh

Those were the days of Covid-19.
What could that mother have been thinking?
Her standing there on the subway platform
Watching blue police hands on the brown body
Of her son, hands that were not the brown hands
That held him at his birth? What was she hoping
Would happen with her words? Was she hoping
Her words would have power, would activate ancient magic
That would release her brown son from the blue hands?
Did she think they didn't understand who that boy was
Who was struggling to be set free? Is that why
She kept repeating the words
Like a command,
Like a mantra,
Like a plea?

How many times
Have mothers repeated those words
In other days?
...at the Slave Markets,
...on the plantations,
...at the gravesites,
...in the courtrooms,
...on subway platforms?

Dead sons walking.

PIETÁ

1.
I had an uncle
who went from one side of the country
 the other, but his mother
still followed him until he
came back home to die.
She held him across her lap
like Michelangelo's Mary held Jesus,

His human body, lifeless.
His soul descended into Hell,
battled with death,
winning
on the Third Day.

2.
I had a grandmother
who held off death—to be ageless
as long as she could,
not wanting to precede her
children to the grave,
but not wanting
to bury them either.

3.
It is good that we are not supposed
to choose. The road not taken
by us will be taken by someone else.
No matter what, regret will
sheds its unproductive leaves on Earth,
an even layering. For some,
if we shield our eyes and focus,
we will be able to make out

those famous yellow bricks,
weeds burgeoning in between,
or a Damascus Road.

"DON'T BE DISRESPECTFUL OF THE DEAD"

-for all mothers of lost sons

They said, "Don't be disrespectful of the dead,"
and she tried not to be,
but maybe she was,
when she touched her son's forehead
as he lay asleep in death
because she knew
he wouldn't mind.
She wanted to know if the shape of him
was there still.
But she was distracted
by the coolness of his forehead,
the thinness of his skin,
the sudden translucence of him.

She was trying to remember
if this might be the way
he always felt-
                this hardness of bone,
                without this frigid coolness.

And was this his face-
unfamiliar without the dimples
which formed whenever he smiled at her?

His sudden departure was disrespectful…

no time for her to prepare herself for loss.
No awareness when he was alive,

she should have touched him more.

MAKING A TEE SHIRT QUILT FOR MY BLACK SONS

1.

In step one you collect them one by one.
Beware; they tend to pile up rapidly.
You soon find out that one gives birth to many,
a ruler measuring your child's growth.
Your memories are sweetly stored within them
like faded photographs with rips and frays.
Then one day you realize there are too many,
the closets and the drawers have overflowed.
The shirts, like years, have piled up way too quickly.
Your children have outgrown the ones they loved,
amassed like years your sons have quickly passed,
unaware that you've always been present,
not noticing the cotton of your touch.

2.

In order to not release your sons too soon,
you must progress onto the second step:
You gather shirts, and now with scissors sharp,
then cutting off the excess, leave its heart.
The first cut really is the deepest cut—
you must be careful not to cut too close,
and when the squares are cut, square upon square,
you lay them out to see what goes with what.
You want to have a faultless fit together,
though faded, shrunken, stained, some very used.

3.

The next step is the most important one.
A backing must be chosen to enfold
your sons with dreams of perfect parenthood, .
 a maternal nest of softness you create,
a womb where tags and stiff clothes don't exist.

4.

Now, sandwich cotton batting in-between,
a buffer against the coarseness of this life,
then sew with equal stitches time together,
your fingers pock- marked from quilt needles pushing
through layers of years of thick-headedness,

and finish with a binding that you bless.

5.
At last, the time has come! Release the quilt.
Release the days and hours that you've spent
and pray the seams can hold their lives together
And keep them from the harm the streets might bring,
the dangers from their Blackness, hovering.

DAYCLEAN

1.
When his wife threw the necklace
and the beads scattered past the four corners of the earth,
she was there.
Together
they gathered the pearls and strung them back,
bead upon bead, like when he was in preschool.

When his wife threw the dishes,
registry gifts not yet used,
together
they made a mosaic, and
it was as beautiful
as he thought his marriage would be.

It was not like she didn't prepare her son.
He had witnessed two broken people
trying to love each other
as much as they loved themselves.
But he had never seen this:
a cauldron full of bitterness, rejection, and loss
boiling since her childhood.
In the days and months she spent in their volatile house,
even together
she could not spill this anger into the Abyss.

2.
When she leaves them alone again,
you will give a Benediction:
May you lie in bed
Together,
and be still.
Listen to the clock marking off the past,
ticking, like your own hearts
beating to the next future second
into the space where timeless hope resides.

...

In the Gullah language, morning is
Dayclean,
a better word than dawn. Maybe
a good Word for all of us too,
starting with an Empty Tomb
as our only hope in this broken world-

a new day,
a new opportunity,
another chance

to begin again.

AKNOWLEDGEMENTS

Versions of these poems have appeared in the following publications:

American Diversity Report: *"Gotta Be Grateful"*

Chattanooga Writers Guild 2019 Anthology: *"Dayclean"*

Cutleaf Journal: *"I Was Raised to be Invisible"*

Global Poemic: *"Let Him Go! That's My Son!"*;

Emerge Literary Journal: *"Caul Baby"*; *"To Be a Distant Son"*

iō Literary Journal: *"Not Just to Have the Bluest Eye"*

Last Stanza Poetry Journal: *"Inheritance"*

Penumbraonline.org: *"Making a Quilt for My Black Sons"*

Poets Choice. Ed. Sonthalia, Akshay. 2020. *"He Had a Dream"*

radix: *"The Rainbow Child"*

Salvation South: *"For Dead Molesters Whose Secrets We Kept"*

The Broken Plate: *"The Walnut Street Bridge"*

805 Lit +Art.org: *"The First Time"*